SCHIRMER'S LIBRARY
OF MUSICAL CLASSICS

FRIEDRICH KUHLAU

Sonatinas
For the Piano

Revised and Fingered by

LUDWIG KLEE

Book I contains a Biographical Sketch of the Author by

PHILIP HALE

IN TWO BOOKS

Book I — Library Vol. 52

 Book II — Library Vol. 53

ISBN 0-7935-8914-2

G. SCHIRMER, *Inc.*

DISTRIBUTED BY

HAL•LEONARD®
CORPORATION

7777 W. BLUEMOUND RD. P.O. BOX 13819 MILWAUKEE, WI 53213

Kuhlau, Sonatinas, Vol. II.

Index.

SONATINA.

Op. 88, № 1.

Fingered and phrased by
LUDWIG KLEE.

FR. KUHLAU.

Allegro (♩ = 126)

10970

SONATINA.

Op. 88, Nº 2.

Fingered and phrased by
LUDWIG KLEE.

FR. KUHLAU.

2.

10971 r

Andante cantabile.

Rondo.
Vivace.

SONATINA.

Op. 88. Nº 3.

Fingered and phrased by
LUDWIG KLEE.

FR. KUHLAU.

Allegro con affetto.

10972 r

Fingered and phrased by
LUDWIG KLEE.
Allegro molto.

SONATINA.
Op.88, Nº4.

FR. KUHLAU.

10973

Andante con moto.

10973

SONATINA.

Op. 60, № 1.

Fingered and phrased by
LUDWIG KLEE.

FR. KUHLAU.

10974

Var. 2.

Var. 4.

SONATINA.

Op. 60, № 2.

Fingered and phrased by
LUDWIG KLEE.

FR. KUHLAU.

10975

10975

Var. 2.

Più moto.

Fingered and phrased by
LUDWIG KLEE.

SONATINA.
Op. 60, № 3.

FR. KUHLAU.

10976r

Var.1.

Var.2.

Var.4.

Var.5.

Allegro molto.